Copyright © 2023 by Diya Z.

All rights reserved. No part of this book may be reproduced or transmitted in any form or by any means without permission in writing from the publisher.

www.innovatorspioneers.com

Innovators and Pioneers

Henry Ford

Written by Diane Z.
Illustrated by Aia Sharawy

Henry Ford was born in a small town near Detroit, Michigan, a city he helped transform into the Motor City of the world.

Growing up on a farm, Henry spent his summers helping out with farm work and attended school during the winters.

From a young age, Henry was fascinated by machines. On his 13th birthday, his father gave him a pocket watch. Henry quickly took the watch apart and put it back together, making it work perfectly.

One summer, Henry accompanied his father to Downtown Detroit. Along the way, they passed many different carriages.

Henry saw a steam-propelled carriage for the first time and was fascinated by the sight and sound of this machine.

Henry spent days and nights tinkering with engines in his workshop, and by the age of 15, he had constructed his first internal combustion engine.

Henry left his hometown to work for the largest company in Detroit.

Out of 2,000 employees, nobody knew more about engines than he did.

Henry loved tinkering with car engines, but he also fell in love with his biggest supporter, Clara. He often said, "The greatest day of my life was the day I married Mrs. Ford."

With the help of his friends, Henry's first car was born. It was Detroit's first gasoline-powered car!

Henry drove his car all over town, attracting a big crowd of onlookers.

Building a company was challenging. After Henry's first company failed, he turned to car racing to rebuild his reputation.

He participated in the Sweepstakes race and proved that his car was the fastest in the world.

Eventually, Henry established a new company to build an affordable car for everyone. After countless experiments, he invented the Model T, which became the most iconic car in the world.

To increase efficiency, Henry built the world's first moving assembly line. It reduced the time required to build a car from 12 hours to 33 minutes.

Henry's next car, the Model A, was significantly more powerful, smoother, and sportier. Enthusiasm and demand were so high that 10 million people viewed the new vehicle within the first week.

Soon, the Great Depression struck. Henry found ways for farmers to recycle agricultural products, transforming them into useful items like fuel and construction material.

Henry also encouraged farmers to grow soybeans, which can be turned into food, paint, plastics, and clothing. He even created a car made from soybean plastic.

Henry Ford was admired and loved by many. He embodied the spirit of entrepreneurship, ingenuity, and hard work.

Henry's greatest achievement was changing the face of America and putting the world on wheels.

www.ingramcontent.com/pod-product-compliance
Lightning Source LLC
Chambersburg PA
CBHW041422010526
44119CB00015B/346